I'd Rather Be Right

A MUSICAL REVUE

BY

GEORGE S. KAUFMAN & MOSS HART

LYRICS BY LORENZ HART

RANDOM HOUSE · NEW YORK

THE PHOTOGRAPHS IN THIS BOOK
ARE BY VANDAMM STUDIO

The score of *I'd Rather Be Right,* composed by Richard Rodgers, is published by Chappell & Co., RKO Building, New York City.

ILLUSTRATIONS

I'd Rather Be Right was produced by Sam H. Harris at the Alvin Theatre, New York, on Tuesday night, November 2, 1937, with the following cast:

Peggy Jones...	Joy Hodges
Phil Barker	Austin Marshall
The President of the United States	George M. Cohan
His Secretary	Ralph Glover
The Postmaster General	Paul Parks
The Secretary of the Treasury	Taylor Holmes
The Secretary of State	Marion Green
The Secretary of Labor	Bijou Fernandez
The Secretary of the Navy	David Allman
The Secretary of Agriculture	Robert Bleck
The Secretary of War	Jack Mills
The Secretary of Commerce	Al Atkins
The Secretary of the Interior	Charles McLoughlin
The Attorney-General	Robert Less
The Chief Justice	John Cherry
James B. Maxwell..	Florenz Ames
Federal Theatre Director	Joseph Macaulay
The Judge's Girl	Mary Jane Walsh
Social Security Man	Georgie Tapps
The President's Mother	Marie Louise Dana
A Butler	Joseph Allen
Sistie	Evelyn Mills
Buzzie..	Warren Mills
Tony	Joseph Macaulay
Joe	Joe Verdi
The Acrobats	{ Jack Reynolds / Sol Black }

Radio Announcer, Ice-Cream Vendor, Pick-Up Man, Policeman, Passers-by, Sailors, Photographers, etc.

Singing Girls—Virginia Berger, Cecil Carey, Ruth Clayton, Geraldine Hamilton, Linda Kellogg, Marie Nash, Erminie Randolph, Jane Richardson and Emily Stephenson.

Singing Boys—Charles Bywater, Len Frank, John Fulco, Joe Granville, Jack Kearney, Jack Leslie, William Marel, John McQuade, Bob Spencer, Norman Van Emburgh and Herbert Wood.

Dancing Girls—Jeanette Bradley, Kate Frederic, Ruth Gormley, Georgette Lampsi, Velma Lord, Lili Mann, Austra Neiman, Tina Rigat, Patsy Schenk, Jeanette Lea, Eleanor Witte, Clarise Sitomer and Dorothy Waller.

Dancing Boys—Jack Barnes, Don Cater, Martin Fair, Edward Harrington, Robert Howard, Beau Tilden, Jay Hunter, James Cushman and Fred Nay.

Dave Allman's Band

Stage Manager—Felix Jacoves
Assistant Stage Managers— { John McCahill / Henry Ephron }

Choreography by Charles Weidman, Modern Dances staged by Ned McGurn, Setting by Donald Oenslager, Costumes by Irene Sharaff, Modern Clothes by John Hambleton, Orchestra under the direction of Harry Levant.

SCENES

ACT ONE
Central Park, New York, dusk of a summer evening.

ACT TWO
Central Park, later that evening.

The Fourth of July

ACT ONE

ACT ONE

A corner in Central Park. It is dusk of a summer evening, and the inspiring panorama of the Fifty-ninth Street skyline is in the background. The Sherry-Netherland, the Plaza, Radio City are silhouetted against the deepening night. In the foreground, a tree or two, a path, a bridge, a rock.

Somewhere in the distance a park concert strikes up—the music floats over the scene. Little groups of people come hurrying along the path, on their way to the concert. There is a little inconsequential chatter—"See, I told you. They've started already." . . . "Well, suppose we miss the first minute. It's free, isn't it?"

A park policeman strolls in, happily waving his club to the beat of the music. Then one of those park pick-up men, stabbing at bits of paper and popping them into his bag.

THE POLICEMAN

Hi, Chauncey!

CHAUNCEY
(That being his name)
These Fourth of July concerts drive me crazy.

THE POLICEMAN

What's the matter? Don't you like the Fourth of July?

CHAUNCEY

Listen, if you had to pick up all them banana skins and
Evening Journals, would *you* like the Fourth of July?
(*He goes*)

THE POLICEMAN

(*To an invisible transgressor*)
Hey! Keep off the grass, you! Where do you think
you are—Russia?
(*And he is off to do his duty*)

(*A young man hurries along the path, followed
by his girl. "Come on! Hurry up! It's started already." . . . "I'm hurrying"*)

(*Next come a couple of millionaires, engrossed in
their own troubles*)

FIRST MILLIONAIRE

But with taxes what they are, Jim, a man can't afford
to *make* more than a hundred thousand dollars a year.

SECOND MILLIONAIRE

You know what it's coming to? You're going to have to
live on a hundred thousand a year and *like* it!

4

FIRST MILLIONAIRE

Yes, sir. Communism.
> (*And they've gone*)

> (*Two girls come along the path*)

FIRST GIRL

And what do you think, he has a private room. And when I picked up the napkin, a hundred-dollar bill falls out.

SECOND GIRL

Say!

FIRST GIRL

So I says, "Whee!—Happy days are here again." And he says, "Happy days nothing. It ain't going to be worth anything, anyhow—so what the hell!"
> (*They go on their way, passing a balloon man on the path. His wares unsold, he sighs heavily. A man and a woman, going to the concert, pass him*)

BALLOON MAN

Balloons! Balloons!

THE MAN

No, thanks.

I'D RATHER BE RIGHT

The Woman

(*Bitterly*)

I don't get even a balloon, huh?

(*They disappear; the* Balloon Man *trudges wearily on. Then come two sailors*)

First Sailor

Yes, sir, I was the dumb one. I joined the Navy and my brother went into business. So what's the answer? We're *both* working for the Government.

Second Sailor

Okay, but how about them two dames over there?

First Sailor

All you think of is dames, you dumb cluck!—Where are they?

(*A vendor comes through, wheeling one of those ice-cream pushcarts*)

The Vendor

Ice cream! All kinds of ice cream! Get an ice cream!

(*From another direction come a young man and a young woman, deep in a familiar argument*)

The Young Man

But, darling, you know I'm right about it.

6

I'D RATHER BE RIGHT

THE YOUNG WOMAN

Well, it's not that I care what people think, Ralph; but if I ever have a baby it'll be terrible.

(*The band reaches a climax. There is a salvo of applause in the distance. Then the band picks up anew, with the poignant opening strains of Mendelssohn's "Nocturne." Into the scene stroll another boy and girl. Just an average American boy and girl*)

THE GIRL

Listen! It's Mendelssohn. . . . I love that.

THE BOY

Probably no seats left. Look at the crowd.

THE GIRL

Isn't that lovely, Phil?
(*She hums along with the music*)
How about staying right here? It's even nicer from a distance.

PHIL

All right.
(*Unfolding a couple of newspapers*)
Which will you have—the *Times* or the *Tribune?*

THE GIRL

Which is the softest?

PHIL

Well, I think the rock is softer than either of them, but here you are.

(*He spreads the papers*)

THE GIRL

Thank you.

(*She sits on the rock*)

(*The boy settles himself beside her. There is a moment's pause as they listen to the music*)

Beautiful, isn't it? . . . Don't you love the Fourth of July?

PHIL

(*Dispiritedly*)

It's all right.

THE GIRL

Phil, what's the matter?

PHIL

Oh, nothing.

THE GIRL

Phil, there's something on your mind. I've noticed it all evening.

PHIL

(*Deciding to take the plunge*)

Well, I might as well tell you. I don't get the new job, Peggy. They're not going to open up the other office. They told me today.

8

PEGGY

Oh, darling!

PHIL

(A sigh)

Yah!

PEGGY

But why, Phil? Didn't they give any reason?

PHIL

Oh, it seems they want to wait till they know what's going to happen, or something—to the country. Is the dollar going down, and are prices going up, and is the budget going to be balanced, or what is going to happen?

PEGGY

But I thought things were better.

PHIL

Well, all I know is, they don't know what's going to happen . . . and that means I stay right where I am.

PEGGY

Phil! What a shame!

PHIL

So that's that! It doesn't leave us with much to look forward to, does it?

9

PEGGY

Look! I'm willing to take the chance. I'll marry you, anyhow—right away.

PHIL

It's no good, Peggy. You know what I make.

PEGGY

But what are we going to do, Phil? We can't wait forever.

PHIL

I don't know. It just seems you can't count on anything any more. It takes the heart out of you. Nobody knowing where they're going—what's happening. The budget, the budget! We can't get married until they balance the budget. That's what it comes down to, Peggy. It doesn't make sense, but it's true.

PEGGY

(*Bitterly*)

It isn't the Montagues and the Capulets that keep you apart any more; it's the budget. Romeo and Juliet, and the budget!

PHIL

Yah. . . . Aw, the hell with it . . . everything!

PEGGY

I love you, Phil.

PHIL

A lot of good that does you.

PEGGY

But it does. It makes me very happy, no matter what happens. Look! Put your head in my lap. Close your eyes. And don't think about it any more, darling. Don't think about anything. Just be very quiet and listen to the music.

(*She strokes his head fondly. The music plays softly on, swells to a crescendo, slowly dies again. The boy and girl sit motionless, his head still in her lap, his eyes closed. Then, along the pathway, comes an impressive-looking man. Frock coat, high hat. By any standards, an important personage. He stops, looks uncertainly about*)

THE STRANGER

I beg your pardon. Does this path lead to Seventy-second Street?

PEGGY

I think so. Doesn't it, Phil?

PHIL

Yes, it does. Right along there.

THE STRANGER

Thank you very much.

PHIL

(*Unable to believe his eyes*)
Ah—excuse me, but—aren't you President Roosevelt?

THE STRANGER

Yes, I am.

PEGGY

President Roosevelt!

ROOSEVELT

So they tell me.

PHIL

(*Stunned*)

I couldn't believe it. I thought it must be, but—my goodness!—I can hardly believe it.

ROOSEVELT

I was just taking a little stroll. I live right over in Sixty-fifth Street, you know—when I'm in New York.

PHIL

Yes, 1 know, but—it kind of takes my breath away.

ROOSEVELT

Well, thank you again. 1 just follow that path, eh?

PEGGY

Yes, sir.

ROOSEVELT

Thank you.

PHIL

(*Stopping him*)

Mr. Roosevelt!

ROOSEVELT

Yes?

PHIL

Have—have you got a minute to spare?

ROOSEVELT

Well, I'm on my way home to write my Fourth of July speech.

PHIL

But couldn't you spare just a few moments?

ROOSEVELT

Well—I'm supposed to speak in about an hour. . . . But what can I do for you?

PHIL

Well, this is Miss Jones—Peggy Jones.

ROOSEVELT

How do you do?

PEGGY

How do you do!

PHIL

And my name is Philip Barker.

ROOSEVELT

How do you do?

PHIL

I'm afraid we haven't any right to bother you with our little troubles. . . .

ROOSEVELT

No, no . . . It's quite all right.

PEGGY

You see, Mr. Roosevelt, we've been in love with each other for a long time. But we've both got families, and we've got jobs that don't pay very well—and there doesn't seem to be any way out.

PHIL

The way things are going, Mr. Roosevelt, we just don't know *what* to do.

PEGGY

So we thought if you could tell us what's going to happen to the country—why, it would be a lot of help.

PHIL

Would you, Mr. Roosevelt? Would you *tell* us?

ROOSEVELT

(*Uneasily*)

Ah—did you say *that* was the way to Seventy-second Street?

PHIL

Please, Mr. Roosevelt. We'll never have a chance like this again. Meeting *you*. We don't know *what* to do. . . . We're worried.

ROOSEVELT

You're worried? What do you think *I* am?

PHIL

Well, could you at least tell us if you're ever going to balance the budget?

ROOSEVELT

(*Dryly*)

That's all you want to know, eh? . . . Well, that's quite a story . . . Do you mind if I sit down?

PEGGY

Oh, please do!

PHIL

We'd be delighted.

ROOSEVELT

(*A glance at the newspaper before he sits*)

Ah! Walter Lippmann. Fine!

(*He sits, then faces the boy and girl again*)

So you two young people want to get married, do you?

PEGGY AND PHIL

Yes!

ROOSEVELT

Well, why don't you go ahead and do it, and let *me* worry about the country? That's my job.

PHIL

Yah, but it doesn't work out that way. We can't get
married unless I get a raise, and the Boss won't give me
the raise until he knows what *you're* going to do. He says
you've got to balance the budget before he does anything.

ROOSEVELT

I see. . . . Say, would you like an ice cream? Hey, ice-
cream man! Right over here! Three!

ICE-CREAM MAN

Yes, sir.

PEGGY

My, I never thought I'd be eating ice cream with the
President of the United States.

ROOSEVELT

Say, I never thought I'd be President. . . . Ah, here
we are!
(*Fishing for a coin*)
Keep the change.
(*As he peels off the paper*)
You know, this is the way I like to eat ice cream. At
the White House, we always have to have Garner with
it.
(*He has taken a little red notebook from his
pocket, and now painstakingly makes an entry in
it*)
"Ice cream, twenty-five cents."

PEGGY

Do you write everything you spend in that little book?

ROOSEVELT

I should say I do. This is the budget!

PHIL

Say! So that's the budget.

ROOSEVELT

Yes, sir. You wouldn't think a little bit of a book like this could put the whole country on the bum, would you?

PHIL

May I—see it?

ROOSEVELT

(*Handing it over*)

Sure! . . . Of course, it's not in very good shape just now.

PHIL

(*Reading from the budget as* PEGGY *looks over his shoulder*)

"Two battleships, a hundred and fifty million dollars."

PEGGY

"Ice cream, twenty-five cents."

ROOSEVELT

Yes, sir—that's how the money goes.

(*A snap of the fingers*)

PHIL

(*Handing back the book*)

What do you think, Mr. Roosevelt? Is there a chance of it's ever getting balanced?

PEGGY

It means just everything to us.

ROOSEVELT

Well, I'll tell you, Phil—Peggy—you're the kind of youngsters that I'd like very much to help. But you've got to realize that balancing the budget is a pretty tough job. Let me show you. Say you make eighteen, twenty dollars a week. All right. You get married, and it costs you thirty-five dollars to live. So you're spending more than you earn, aren't you?

PEGGY

Yes, sir.

ROOSEVELT

Well, that's just the way it is with the Government.

PHIL

Yes, sir. That's what my boss is worried about.

ROOSEVELT

Well, your boss is right.

PEGGY

(*Eagerly*)

Well, then?

ROOSEVELT

(*Summing it up*)

Well, that's the situation. The Government couldn't get married—I can tell you that.

PHIL

(*A deep sigh*)

That's that, then. I'll just go on making that eighteen a week, and that'll be the end of it. Honest, Mr. Roosevelt, it's pretty tough.

ROOSEVELT

I know it is, Phil. Don't think I haven't thought about it a lot. This country's full of youngsters like you—eager, willing to work—and you've got a right to expect what you're after. A home, and kids, and enough to get along on. And I'll tell you something—we've got to give it to you. Because you're the people that count. You young ones. You're America . . . not us old fellows sitting behind desks. . . . Yes, sir—I've thought about it a lot.

PEGGY

But what's going to happen, Mr. Roosevelt? How long have we got to wait?

ROOSEVELT

I don't know. I've been trying all kinds of things since I became President. But it's no easy job. These are tough times, you know, all over the world.

PHIL

I know it, Mr. Roosevelt—but isn't there *anything* you can do?

ROOSEVELT

I wish there were. . . .
(*Regarding them*)
You know, I like you two, and I'd like to help you. Yes, sir, I'd like to help you.
(*A pause*)
Tell me, if I could balance the budget, that'd help, huh? You'd get that new job?

PHIL

Yes, I would. It'd be wonderful.

PEGGY

(*Tremulous with excitement*)
Mr. Roosevelt, *will* you? Will you balance the budget?

ROOSEVELT

Kids, I'll tell you what I *will* do. I'll *try*. I'll try real hard and see if I can do it.

PEGGY

Oh, Mr. Roosevelt!

ROOSEVELT

Because I want to see you two married, if it's the last thing I do as President.

20

PEGGY

Mr. Roosevelt, how wonderful!

PHIL

Peggy, do you hear that?

PEGGY

Darling!
(*They embrace*)
Thank you, Mr. Roosevelt. Thank you.

ROOSEVELT

Now, wait a minute. It isn't balanced yet, you know.

(*Enter* McINTYRE, *the President's secretary*)

McINTYRE

Mr. President!

ROOSEVELT

Yes, McIntyre?

McINTYRE

Are you ready for the Cabinet?

ROOSEVELT

I should say I am! I want to talk to them. Send them in.
(*As* McINTYRE *goes*)
You two stick right with me—I'm going to take this up right now.

McIntyre

(*Returning*)
The Cabinet!

(*And the* Cabinet *enters—all ten of them. Singing, of course—it's a well-known fact that the* Cabinet *always sings when it gets together for a meeting*)

Cabinet

We're a homogeneous Cabinet,
And you can't tell us apart.
From the way we're grouped,
You'd think we'd trouped
With Rupert D'Oyly Carte.

But—
Perkins and Farley,
And Farley and Perkins
Know all of your business and all of its
    workin's—
Do Perkins and Farley,
And Farley and Perkins—
Do Perkins and Farley and Hull.

Roosevelt

Gentlemen, I want you to meet two young friends of mine— Miss Peggy Jones and Mr. Philip Barker.

(*There is an exchange of greetings*)

The Postmaster-General!

FARLEY
(As the music strikes up again)
I keep my popularity forever hale and hearty
By finding jobs for everyone in the Democratic
    Party.
A job for every uncle and a job for every niece—
I give a job for every vote, and how the votes
    increase!
Some guys are such good voters they get twenty
    jobs apiece!
    Three cheers for the land of F. D.!

ROOSEVELT
The Secretary of Labor!

MISS PERKINS
All of these strikes keep a girl on her toes;
I've barely got time to powder my nose.
I fight for the workmen and fight for the bosses,
And the more that I fight, the bigger their losses.
It would help the whole thing a great deal, I
    suppose,
If I gave it all up and just powdered my nose.

ROOSEVELT
The Secretary of the Treasury!

I'D RATHER BE RIGHT

MORGENTHAU
I'm quite a busy man right now—
I'm Secretary Morgenthau.
You may have heard that I attend
To what you call the money end.
Since first this land of ours began,
I am its top financial man.
I have achieved, you must admit,
The biggest goddam deficit!

ROOSEVELT
And these are the rest of the boys. This is Secretary—
ah—I'm sorry, I never can remember your name.

SWANSON
Nobody knows who I am—

CABINET
And nobody gives a damn!

Perkins and Farley and Hull—
We meet twice a week and it's dull.
Morgenthau, Cummings and Ick-es,
We'd like to give all of them mick-eys.
Roper and Wallace, and all of the rest
Are unknown in the East and the same in the
    West.
But Perkins and Farley,
And Farley and Perkins,

Know all of your business and all of its
    workin's—
Do Perkins and Farley,
And Farley and Perkins,
Yes, Perkins and Farley,
And Farley and Perkins,
Do Perkins and Farley and Hull.

(*The finish finds the* CABINET *standing around
the traditional long table, which has been carried
in under cover of the music. The Cabinet members' portfolios miraculously turn into chairs.*
PHIL *and* PEGGY, *guided by the* PRESIDENT, *have
taken their places at his side*)

ROOSEVELT

Gentlemen, the Cabinet is in session. Now, first . . .

FARLEY

(*On his feet at once*)
Excuse me, Mr. President, but there's something I've
got to take up right away.

ROOSEVELT

Make it short, Jim. I've got something to take up myself.

FARLEY

Well, I'll make it as short as I can. Gentlemen, we
have got to create more jobs for deserving Democrats.
    (*A groan from the* CABINET)

25

ROOSEVELT

Jim, how many deserving Democrats *are* there?

FARLEY

You keep forgetting, Frank, how much they deserve for putting us in again.

HULL

Mr. President!

ROOSEVELT

The Secretary of State.

HULL

I hope I shall not be requested to place any more deserving Democrats in the State Department. Mr. Farley's last appointee did not know Brazil from brassières. In fact, we got in a good deal of trouble with Brazil on that account.

FARLEY

All right, we all make mistakes, Cordell. Besides, it was only Brazil. . . . Now this fellow . . .
  (*He has a letter in his hand*)
. . . is Chairman of the Fourth Assembly District in Seattle. He wants to be Collector of the Port of New York. How about it?

ROOSEVELT

But we've *got* a Collector of the Port of New York.

FARLEY

Not in Seattle.

ROOSEVELT

But why give him New York? Why not make him Collector of the Port of Seattle?

FARLEY

No, no—a fellow in New Orleans has got that.

ROOSEVELT

I see. You haven't given *my* job away yet, have you, Jim?

FARLEY

Well, Frank, we've got to take care of the boys. Look what we did in New York. Started a World's Fair, just to give Grover Whalen a job. Now, I've got a short list here that have been Democrats ever since Thomas Jefferson.

(*The short list turns out to be six feet long*)

ROOSEVELT

Well, if they've waited that long, they can wait a little longer. There's something *I've* got to take up.

MORGENTHAU

Mr. President!

ROOSEVELT

(*Wearily*)

The Secretary of the Treasury.

27

MORGENTHAU

(*A trifle sheepishly*)

Mr. President, I'm running short of money again.

ROOSEVELT

Now, Henry—what happened to that money I gave you last week?

MORGENTHAU

I spent it.

ROOSEVELT

Three hundred million dollars? That ought to last you more than a week, Henry.

MORGENTHAU

I know, but somehow it goes. Do you think you could let me have . . .

(*He summons all his charm*)

. . . another couple of hundred millions? I'll try to make it last out the week.

ROOSEVELT

No, Henry, I cannot. And, gentlemen, that's just what I want to talk to you about. . . . Mr. Cummings, stop drawing pictures and listen to me.

HULL

Mr. President.

ROOSEVELT

Yes, Mr. Hull. . . . What is it?

28

I'D RATHER BE RIGHT

HULL

I just want to suggest that if we can hurry things up, why, the new Marx Brothers picture opens today and we could all go and see it.

("Yes!" . . . "Oh, that's fine!")

ROOSEVELT

No, no, no. I want everybody's attention, please.

(A chorus of disappointment)

You can see the second show. . . . Now I've already introduced you to these two young people, haven't I? Now, you're not going to like this. It's something that we said we weren't ever going to talk about again, but I've got a special reason. I've *got* to talk about it. Gentlemen, it's the budget.

(A great chorus of "Aw's")

I know, but wait till I tell you. This boy and girl are in love with each other, and they want to get married. But they can't get married unless Phil gets a raise, and he won't get the raise unless we balance the budget.

MORGENTHAU

Well, they're awfully nice young people, Mr. President, but you know as well as I do that we *can't* balance the budget.

ROOSEVELT

Now, wait a minute. We've *got* to balance it. You just listen to these two young people and see if you don't feel as I do.

29

(*He turns to the youngsters*)

Phil, Peggy—I want you to tell the Cabinet your story. And, gentlemen, if this doesn't make you want to balance the budget, I don't know what will.

(*And, with the* CABINET *as audience,* PHIL *bursts right into song. It is a sentimental recounting of the thrills and delights that were his on the immortal occasion when he and* PEGGY *were first introduced to one another. This is the burden of his refrain—the refrain itself, as a matter of fact:*)

"Have you met Miss Jones?"
Someone said as we shook hands.
She was just Miss Jones to me.
Then I said, "Miss Jones,
You're a girl who understands;
I'm a man who must be free."
And all at once I lost my breath,
And all at once was scared to death,
And all at once I owned the earth and sky!
Now I've met Miss Jones,
And we'll keep on meeting till we die—
Miss Jones and I.

(PEGGY, *not to be outdone, responds in kind. It seems that she was thrilled, too. And so is the* CABINET. *The members thereof listen attentively, and are obviously moved when it is all over*)

ROOSEVELT

(*When* PHIL *and* PEGGY *are finished*)

Well, gentlemen?

MORGENTHAU

Mr. President, if we don't do something about this, we're just a bunch of dirty Republicans!

FARLEY

(*Choked up*)

He's right, Frank. Let those Democrats wait.

MISS PERKINS

As a woman, perhaps I can speak for all of us. We *must* balance the budget.

(*She wipes away a furtive tear*)

ROOSEVELT

Thank you, Miss Perkins. . . . I take it for granted that you all feel the same way.

MORGENTHAU

Of course we do.

HULL

We just can't talk.

ROOSEVELT

(*To* PHIL *and* PEGGY)

There! Is this a nice little Government or isn't it?

PEGGY AND PHIL

Oh, yes, Mr. Roosevelt! It's wonderful!

ROOSEVELT

(*To the* CABINET)

Now then, I'm open for suggestions. *How* are we going
to balance the budget?

(*He looks around the table, hopefully*)

SECRETARY OF THE NAVY

(*Belligerently*)

Can't cut the Navy!

SECRETARY OF COMMERCE

Mustn't touch Commerce!

FARLEY

Don't look at *me!*

ROOSEVELT

(*Reproachfully*)

Now, gentlemen, that wasn't what I meant at all. All
I meant was—what *new taxes* can you think of?

(*Great relief all around, naturally.* "Well!" . . .
"*Why didn't you say so?*" . . . "*That's different!*")

FARLEY

(*Rubbing his hands*)

Hot dog! New taxes, boys! Wheeee!

ROOSEVELT

Jim, you ought to be able to think of something. What about the Post-office Department? How about some hundred-dollar stamps?

FARLEY

Frank, that gives me an idea. Suppose every letter has to be sent air mail? That would double the revenue from stamps. If it only goes from the Bronx to Brooklyn, it has to go air mail.

ROOSEVELT

No. Nobody in the Bronx has got anything important enough to send air mail.

FARLEY

They wouldn't *go* air mail—we'd just send them the regular way. But it would double the revenue.

ROOSEVELT

No, no, Jim. That wouldn't be honest.

FARLEY

Oh! I thought you were talking about taxes.

MISS PERKINS

Mr. President.

ROOSEVELT

The Secretary of Labor.

33

MISS PERKINS

I just thought of something.

ROOSEVELT

Really?

MISS PERKINS

The Government owns a lot of property, doesn't it? The White House, and the Capitol. All those postoffices. It owns property all over the country.

ROOSEVELT

(*Judicially*)

Well?

MISS PERKINS

Well, it doesn't pay any taxes at all. So why don't we just tax the Government for that property, and that would give us all the money we need! Let's tax the day-lights out of 'em!

ROOSEVELT

(*Controlling himself*)

Look, Frances, you just relax for a while.

(*He turns to* PHIL *and* PEGGY)

You know, sometimes I think a woman's place is in the home.

MORGENTHAU

Mr. President, the important thing about a tax is that people mustn't *feel* it. Now, how about a Government pickpocket, in plain clothes, that goes up behind a man and just quietly slips his hand into his pocket?

34

(He pantomimes the procedure)
He'd just take what he'd happen to find there.
(Approval from CABINET: *"Oh, yes—fine!")*

ROOSEVELT

No-o. The Supreme Court wouldn't stand for it. You know how conservative they are.

MORGENTHAU

Let's not *tell* the Supreme Court. Why do we have to tell them everything?

ROOSEVELT

Well, you know what happened the last time we tried to slip something over.

MORGENTHAU

That's because you told it to Congress and it got into the newspapers.

ROOSEVELT

Now, Henry, you know I haven't bothered with Congress in four years.

MORGENTHAU

Well, the important thing is not to let the *Supreme Court* know.

ROOSEVELT

Say, I never thought of that. Mr. Cummings, take a law. "It is hereby enacted, this day and date, that the United States Government . . ."

(But he gets no further. From out of the bushes, from behind rocks, pop the nine members of the Supreme Court)

THE SUPREME COURT
(Gleefully)
Ah, no! No, you don't! Oh, no!

THE CHIEF JUSTICE
Remember, Frankie—no matter how you slice it, it's still the Supreme Court. . . . Oh, no!
(And with another gleeful laugh, they disappear)

ROOSEVELT
(Definitely piqued)
Why don't they stand up and fight like a man?

PEGGY
Does that mean there's no way out, Mr. Roosevelt? Isn't there *anything* you can do?

ROOSEVELT
No, I'll be *darned* if I'm going to let the Supreme Court or *anything* keep you two from getting married. . . . Come on, gentlemen, let's put our heads together. Is there anything at all we haven't taxed?

MORGENTHAU
(Thinking hard)
No, there isn't. There isn't a thing.

MR. ROOSEVELT: "CUMMINGS, TAKE A LAW!"
THE SUPREME COURT: "OH, NO! NO, YOU DON'T! OH, NO!"

FARLEY

Isn't there anything we could sell? Do we need Baltimore?

HULL

How about a tax on shaving? That'd run into money.

ROOSEVELT

No, no. Every man in the country would raise a beard, and they'd all look like Chief Justice Hughes. I couldn't stand that—I'd rather not balance the budget.

PEGGY

Mr. Roosevelt, do you mind if *I* make a suggestion?

ROOSEVELT

Sure. We're not getting anywhere.

PEGGY

Well, what about the women? I was reading the other day about all the money that women spend on beauty treatments—you know, rouge and lipstick, and face creams. And it came to three billion dollars a year!

ROOSEVELT

Well?

PEGGY

Well, is that all taxed, Mr. Roosevelt?

ROOSEVELT

Is it, Henry?

MORGENTHAU

Yes, that's taxed, too.

ROOSEVELT

(*To* PEGGY)
There you are.

PEGGY

Well, I—just wondered.

ROOSEVELT

Too bad. . . . How much did you say they spend?

PEGGY

It said three billion dollars.

ROOSEVELT

Every year, huh?

PEGGY

That's what it said.

MISS PERKINS

Yes, that's true. Cosmetics alone are pretty near a billion.

ROOSEVELT

Three billion dollars. If we could lay our hands on that, it would pretty nearly do the trick. . . . Say, I've got an idea.

(*Everyone leans forward eagerly*)

And the Supreme Court can't touch it, either. Because this isn't against the law, or the Constitution, or anything.

FARLEY

What is it?

ROOSEVELT

Yes, sir—I think I've got it. How about asking the women of this country to give up beauty for one year, give the money to the Government instead, and balance the budget?

HULL

Say, that's an idea.

MORGENTHAU

Why didn't we think of that before?

FARLEY

Yes!

PEGGY

But, Mr. Roosevelt, do you think they'll do it?

ROOSEVELT

Why not? Look what the women did in Italy—gave up their wedding rings, didn't they?

HULL

Yes, that's so.

FARLEY

I don't think it's too much to ask. I've grown bald in the service of my country.

39

ROOSEVELT

Come on now, gentlemen, what about the women?
Are we going to ask them to give up beauty?

MISS PERKINS

I wouldn't have to, would I? Government employee?

ROOSEVELT

Really, Frances—are we going to balance the budget or
aren't we?

MISS PERKINS

Very well. Only I don't see how you're going to make
them do it.

ROOSEVELT

I'll make them. You watch me.

ROPER

It's a tough job, Mr. President.

ROOSEVELT

It's legal, isn't it?

CUMMINGS

Yes.

ROOSEVELT

That's all I have to know.

HULL

But what are you going to *do,* Mr. President? How are you going to do it?

ROOSEVELT

I'll tell you how I'm going to do it. A fireside talk.

THE CABINET

A-ah!

ROOSEVELT

Sure! You didn't think we'd all be here for a second term, did you? What did it?—My fireside talks!

(*He turns to* PEGGY)

Did you know I was the Number One Personality on the air? It has nothing to do with my being President, either. It's just something I've got. I don't know what it is, but I've got it.

(*In the twinkling of an eye the Cabinet table has been whisked away. In its place stands a beautiful fireside, complete with logs and a comfortable blaze. At the same time a radio man brings a microphone into place; stands ready, watch in hand*)

THE RADIO MAN

Okay, Mr. President.

41

ROOSEVELT

(*To* PHIL *and* PEGGY, *with a wink*)

Watch me pour it on.

MORGENTHAU

(*Consulting a slip of paper handed him by the* RADIO MAN)

Ladies and gentlemen of the radio audience, there has been a slight re-arrangement in your radio program. Instead of Stoopnagle and Budd, you will now hear the President of the United States.

ROOSEVELT

(*Advancing to the microphone*)

My friends! And this time, when I say "My Friends," I mean my lady friends, the women of America. This is a special appeal directed to you ladies. I've got a little favor to ask. I've been thinking a lot about you ladies lately. I think that American women are the most beautiful in the entire world. I remember quite some years ago, when a cousin of mine, Theodore Roosevelt, was President, I used to be invited to the White House receptions, and I'll never forget how beautiful the women were. I don't know where Elizabeth Arden or Helena Rubinstein were in those days, but I do know that without rouge, lipstick, or mascara, or any of those things, those women were beautiful. Not that you aren't beautiful today, mind you, but there is something about a woman's *natural* beauty—well, this is what I want to say to you. It so happens that we've been having a little trouble, for the past five or six years, balancing the budget, as it's called. And since you ladies are just as beautiful *without* all those face creams and things, I wondered if you wouldn't be willing to give those all up for *one year,* and send that money to the Government instead. And if you'll do that, here's what the Government will do for you: we'll send each and every one of you a little emblem that you can wear, to show that you are helping to balance the budget. It happens that we've got left over, from an experiment we tried, quite a number of lovely little Blue Eagles, and they'll look very nice on you. Not only that, but every man in the Democratic Party— and I guess you know how many there are, after that last election—will be asked to go out only with those of you who are letting your natural beauty speak for itself, and wearing a Blue Eagle. So I want all of you ladies who have the true American spirit, and who would like to meet some nice Democrats, to sit down tonight and send your checks to Secretary Morgenthau—M-o-r-g-e-n-t-h-a-u —Washington, D. C. And let me tell you, ladies—if you've never gone out with a registered Democrat, you've never gone out at all. Good night, my friends.

> (*There is a chorus of praise from the* CABINET. *The* PRESIDENT *travels down the line, shaking hands and beaming. Simultaneously, the fireplace and the microphone are whisked away. As the congratulations are at their height, there comes a warning*

*blast of trumpets from the orchestra. And then
the deluge. On stalk the women of America, right
out of Elizabeth Arden's. They are wearing the
typical Elizabeth Arden nun-like costume, and are
followed by a battalion of male beauty specialists.
The latter have the little waxed mustaches of their
kind. and are carrying hair curlers, almost as
though they were bayonets)*

(And this is their song)

> Not for a year,
> Not for a month,
> Not for a day
> Will we give beauty away.
> Not for a man,
> Not for a flag,
> Not for the earth—
> That's what our beauty is worth.
> We'll give up our sons for battle,
> We'll give up our husbands for less;
> But feminine drums will rattle
> For feminine make-up and dress.
> Not for a year,
> Not for a month,
> Not for a day
> Will we give beauty away.

> When a man meets a man on a train,
> He doesn't talk of crops and rain.

"IT HAPPENS THAT WE'VE GOT LEFT OVER, FROM AN EXPERIMENT WE
TRIED, QUITE A NUMBER OF LOVELY LITTLE BLUE EAGLES"

I'D RATHER BE RIGHT

When a man sees a musical show
He likes the first or second row.
And the man on the train
Who won't speak of the rain,
And the man at the show
In the very first row,
No matter what place they're in
Are brothers under the skin!

You take your brains,
You take your gold,
I'll take my beauty,
And take and take and take.
While I take pains
Not to grow old,
I'll take my beauty
And make and make and make.
Beware, rich girls,
Smart girls, beware
Of a fancy rag, a shapely bone,
A lovely hank o' hair.
I can't sew a stitch,
Can't bake a cake,
But watch this cutie
Take the cake for beauty;
Take and take and take!

*(The number is carried to a crescendo of indigna-
tion. With a final ultimatum to let beauty alone,*

45

the procession departs. MR. ROOSEVELT, PHIL *and* PEGGY *are left to pick up the pieces*)

PHIL

Looks pretty hopeless, doesn't it?

ROOSEVELT

No, no. I've faced bigger problems than this. I haven't solved them, but I've faced them.

(*Whereupon a* BALLOON VENDOR *enters, carrying a full stock of colored balloons*)

BALLOON MAN

Balloons, balloons! Want to buy a balloon?

PHIL

No, thank you.
(*He takes a second look and is considerably surprised*)
Why, Mr. Maxwell! Whatever are you doing selling balloons?

MAXWELL

(*A ragged and unshaven figure*)
How do you do, Philip?

PHIL

Mr. Roosevelt, may 1 introduce Mr. James B. Maxwell—my boss.

(*Greetings are exchanged*)
And—Miss Jones.
(*Again greetings*)
Mr. Maxwell, what are you doing selling balloons?

MAXWELL

(*Restraining himself*)
I am selling balloons, Philip, because your friend there
has made it impossible for me to make a nickel out of the
wholesale furniture business.

ROOSEVELT

Just a minute—did you say this was your boss, Phil?

PHIL

Yes, sir.

ROOSEVELT

Well, this may be the end of all our troubles. Mr. Maxwell, Phil has told me that he can't get married to Peggy
here because you're not going to open up a new place and
give him a raise. That right?

MAXWELL

That's right.

ROOSEVELT

Well, now! You look like a mighty nice man to me,
Mr. Maxwell, and I'm sure you'd like to see these two
young people get married and be happy. Wouldn't you?

MAXWELL

Yes.

ROOSEVELT

So why don't you open up the new place and give Phil his raise? Come now, Mr. Maxwell—why not?

MAXWELL

Why not, huh? Philip, hold these balloons, and Mr. Roosevelt, take off your glasses.
(*He starts to strip off his coat*)

PHIL

(*Holding him back*)
Now, wait a minute, Mr. Maxwell—please.

ROOSEVELT

(*Puzzled*)
What did I say?

PEGGY

All he said was, why don't you open up the new place, Mr. Maxwell.

ROOSEVELT

That's all I said. My, some people are touchy.

MAXWELL

Touchy? You've got me selling balloons, Mr. Roosevelt, and I'm touchy, huh? Well, Mr. Roosevelt, I will try to tell you why I'm not opening up the new place.

48

Last year, in my business, I made two hundred thousand
dollars. . . . If you please . . .

    (*He hands* ROOSEVELT *the balloons to hold*)

Yes, sir, two hundred thousand dollars. Now then, first
we have the corporation tax—

    (*He breaks a balloon with his lighted cigarette*)

—the excess profits tax—

    (*Another balloon goes*)

—the undivided surplus tax—

    (*Bang*)

—social security tax—

    (*Bang*)

—workmen's liability tax—

    (*Bang*)

—real property tax—

    (*Bang*)

—personal property tax—

    (*Bang*)

—license tax—

    (*Bang*)

—franchise tax—

    (*Bang*)

—sales tax—

    (*Bang*)

—unemployment insurance tax—

    (*Bang*)

—Federal old age tax—

    (*Bang*)

—capital stock tax—
   (*Bang*)
—and the stock transfer tax—
   (*Bang*)
Now you see, Mr. Roosevelt, what I have got left. All right. But I have to *live*, Mr. Roosevelt. So I draw out some money from the corporation to live on, and it starts all over again. Federal income tax—
   (*Bang*)
—State income tax—
   (*Bang*)
—County tax—
   (*Bang*)
—municipal tax—
   (*Bang*)
—poll tax—
   (*Bang*)
—personal property tax—
   (*Bang*)
—real property tax—
   (*Bang*)
—sales tax—
   (*Bang*)
—unemployment tax—
   (*Bang*)
—social security tax—
   (*Bang*)
—school tax—
   (*Bang*)

—gross receipts tax—
(*Bang*)
—gasoline tax—
(*Bang*)
—gift tax—
(*Bang*)
—and the admissions tax—
(*Bang*)
(*There is now but a single balloon remaining*)
And finally, Mr. Roosevelt, thank God, I die! But just in case 1 have anything left, Mr. Roosevelt, the *inheritance* tax.
(*And he punctures the final balloon*)
And that's why I'm not opening up the new place, Mr. Roosevelt. Not only that, but that's why I'm selling balloons, Mr. Roosevelt. And now I haven't even a balloon left. In fact, I'm lucky to have my pants on. Good night!

(*And he goes out. There is quite a long pause after his departure.* PHIL *and* MR. ROOSEVELT *look at each other*)

ROOSEVELT

Well, I guess he isn't going to open up the new place.
(*Enter* CHAUNCEY, *the pick-up man. He is whistling gaily*)

CHAUNCEY

(*Seeing the balloon fragments, and addressing* MR. ROOSEVELT)
Out of the way, buddy!

ROOSEVELT

I'm very sorry.

CHAUNCEY

(*On his knees*)

What do you think we've got ash-cans for? Littering up the whole place . . . and then I have to pick it up.

ROOSEVELT

You think *you've* got troubles, huh? I'll tell you what— I'll trade you right now.

CHAUNCEY

(*Who can't be bothered with these strange people*)

That's the trouble with this country. Too many foreigners.

(*He goes*)

ROOSEVELT

(*Looking after him*)

The trouble with this country is that I don't know what the trouble with the country *is*.

(*Into the scene—suddenly, and for no apparent reason—there stroll a dozen or more beautiful girls, in gay musical-comedy costumes that were never designed for just strolling through a park. With them comes a rather seedy but artistic-looking individual. It turns out to be a band of strolling players, and the seedy-looking individual is their director. He surveys the somewhat startled trio*)

52

I'D RATHER BE RIGHT

DIRECTOR

Pardon me, are you people doing anything?

ROOSEVELT

Huh? Why—no.

DIRECTOR

Well, do you mind if we give a show here?

ROOSEVELT

A show?

DIRECTOR

We're the Federal Theatre, Unit No. 864.

ROOSEVELT

Oh! Well . . . We *are* kind of busy. . . .

DIRECTOR

Can't help that. Whenever we see three people together, we're supposed to give a show. We're the Federal Theatre.

ROOSEVELT

Well, if it's the law . . . Say, you've got quite an organization, haven't you?

DIRECTOR

Oh, this is only one unit. It's pretty hard to go any place these days without tripping over the Federal Theatre. Went into my own bathroom the other day, and there they were!

53

ROOSEVELT

What were they doing—taking a bath?

DIRECTOR

No, my wife was in the tub and they were giving a performance of *She Stoops to Conquer*.

ROOSEVELT

Right in front of your wife?

DIRECTOR

Yes, indeed. But as long as the Government pays for it, it's all right with me.

ROOSEVELT

Tell me—I suppose all this costs the Government a good deal of money, huh?

DIRECTOR

Certainly does. This thing we're going to show you now cost six hundred and seventy-five thousand dollars.

ROOSEVELT

Six hundred and seventy-five thousand dollars! Say— Franklin D. Ziegfeld. . . . Well, so long as it spreads the idea of good government—I suppose this show *is* about the government, huh?

DIRECTOR

Oh, no. No, indeed. This is called *Spring in Vienna*.

ROOSEVELT

Spring in Vienna. Well, that sounds nice. What happens?

DIRECTOR

Nothing happens. It's just Spring in Vienna.

ROOSEVELT

Just Spring in Vienna, for six hundred and seventy-five thousand dollars?

DIRECTOR

That's right. All ready, girls.

(*And they go into it. Moreover, it seems the* DIRECTOR *was quite right about it's being just Spring in Vienna. For this is the lyric:*)

It's spring in Vienna,
And spring when I sing;
It's spring in the hilltops,
And spring in the spring.
It's spring in Vienna,
And spring in my heart,
The spring in the breeze
Says we'll never part;
It's spring in Vienna,
So I and Frederica
Won't part.

Lilacs in blossom,
Dew on the grass;

55

Knockwurst on table,
Beer in the glass.
I'm happy when a
Spring starts to start.
Spring in Vienna
Says we won't part.
Stay, Frederica, my heart.

(*And so on, through several choruses, a ballet
dance, etc. When it's all over, the company pauses
for approval*)

DIRECTOR

There you are, sir. *Spring in Vienna.* How did you like
it?

ROOSEVELT

Six hundred and seventy-five thousand dollars, huh?
That was quite a spring they had over there.

DIRECTOR

Well, of course, we just did this on a shoestring.

ROOSEVELT

A shoestring, huh? Well, do me a favor, will you? Do
the next one at the Centre Theatre and let the Rockefellers pay for it. They've got more money than the Government, anyhow.

DIRECTOR

(*Enchanted at the idea*)

The Rockefellers! Say! . . . Hurry up, girls!

(*And they hurry away—to 26 Broadway, doubtless.*
Mr. Roosevelt *looks after them; sighs deeply*)

ROOSEVELT
(*Bringing out the budget and entering the new
expenditure*)
Six hundred and seventy-five thousand dollars. Well,
you can't take it with you. . . . Of course, there's *one*
way the budget could be balanced—just like that!

PEGGY
What is it?

ROOSEVELT
(*Reconsidering*)
Oh, what's the use? They wouldn't do it.

PHIL
Who? What?

PEGGY
Who wouldn't do it?

ROOSEVELT
The Supreme Court. All they would have to do is *say*
the budget is balanced, and that would be that. They're
supreme, aren't they? Whatever they say goes. God
knows, I found *that* out.

PHIL
Say! Have you ever *asked* them to do it?

ROOSEVELT

They wouldn't do anything for me. They don't like me. And I didn't do anything to *them*. I only tried to get 'em out.

PEGGY

It's too bad, isn't it?

ROOSEVELT

(*Justifying himself*)

Well, how would you like it if, every time you tried to do something, somebody said, "No, no!"

(*He imitates the tone of a small boy*)

I haven't got anything against 'em personally, but they're so mean to me.

(*Again he imitates them*)

"No, no." *You* heard 'em.

PEGGY

But look! Suppose you were very nice to them—told 'em you were sorry, and said some lovely things to them —don't you think they might do you a little favor, and declare the budget balanced?

ROOSEVELT

I hate to ask a favor of those old . . .

(*He gropes for a word*)

PEGGY

Well, I guess we might as well give up, then. We're never going to get married.

ROOSEVELT

You *are* going to get married. . . . All right—I'll *ask* them. I said I'd die before I asked a favor of 'em—but I'll ask them.

PEGGY

Oh, thank you, Mr. Roosevelt.

PHIL

When'll you do it?

ROOSEVELT

Right now. This very minute.

PEGGY

(*Looking around*)
But where are they?

ROOSEVELT

Oh, they're around—in the bushes and behind rocks.

PHIL

How do you make them come out?

ROOSEVELT

I'll make them come out. Stand over there and be very quiet.

(*He starts to stroll around with elaborate unconcern, at the same time whistling idly. Then suddenly he stops short and speaks in a loud voice*)
I am going to pass a law—

59

(*Immediately, out from behind the rocks and bushes, pop those nine gray heads*)

THE SUPREME COURT

Oh, no! No, you don't. Oh, no!

ROOSEVELT

(*Very sweetly*)

Hello, boys.

(*They look at him suspiciously*)

I'm not going to pass any laws. I just wanted to talk to you. Come on out in the open for a minute.

(*They hang back*)

Oh, come on! Honest, I'm not going to do anything.

(*They come a step or two forward*)

My, but you're all looking well. What a lot of handsome men you are!

(*They look at each other, still suspicious*)

Come on a little farther. You know, you boys have got me all wrong. I think you're fine. I like you. Why, every morning when I wake up, I look out of the White House window and see that lovely new building of yours—and I say to myself, "Isn't it nice to have those lovely, nine old . . ."

(*He catches himself*)

". . . those lovely nine men up there, looking after everything." I tell you, this is a pretty lucky country. Now, I wonder if I can ask you boys to do me a little favor.

I'D RATHER BE RIGHT

THE SUPREME COURT
(*In unison and without hesitation*)
No!

ROOSEVELT
(*Very sweetly*)
Don't you even want to hear what it is?

THE SUPREME COURT
No!

ROOSEVELT
(*Controlling himself with difficulty*)
Now, look. . . . If you came to me and asked *me* a favor, I'd do it. . . . Ask me a favor. Anything.

THE CHIEF JUSTICE
All right. Go jump in the lake.

ROOSEVELT
(*Breaking out*)
Now, you boys are not being very nice.

THE CHIEF JUSTICE
If I were you, Mr. President, I would not talk about being nice.

ROOSEVELT
Why not? What have I done?

THE CHIEF JUSTICE
Oh, nothing. Nothing at all. Only issued a statement calling us nine old men, that's all. So you needn't come sucking around *now*, Mr. President.

I'D RATHER BE RIGHT

ROOSEVELT
Now, hold on a minute. I didn't mean that.

THE CHIEF JUSTICE
Oh, yes, you did! "Horse and buggy days," eh? "Old fogies," eh? Well, that's how much you know.

(They all put their fingers in their mouths and whistle, shrilly. From behind the bushes, rocks and trees come nine young girls—and such girls! Their costumes are scanty, to say the least—in fact they look as though they had just stepped out of the floor show of the "Paradise." They link arms with the nine JUSTICES *and gaily explain the why and wherefore of it all)*

THE GIRLS
No money in this world ever budges
Our judges.
When duty calls, their duty is done.
We patriotic ladies know them,
And show them,
A little bit of constitutional fun.
The way they always want to be lawful
Is awful—
Their fortitude is second to none.
They love their Constitution—
We know it,
And show it,

By giving them some constitutional fun.
Judge John Marshall
Was most impartial—
From law he'd never retrench;
But after duty,
He liked a cutie
To soothe his callous from the bench.
Though Presidents may try to coerce them,
Disperse them,
They've won their fight before it's begun.
And we're the girls they never say "No" to,
But go to
To get a little constitutional fun,
And they deserve some constitutional fun.

(*And then into their dance—and what a dance!
Cartwheels, somersaults, everything. Then, with
their girls, they disappear right into the bushes
again*)

ROOSEVELT
(*Looking after them*)
You know, if I'd suggested putting six new *girls* on
the Bench, I'll bet they'd have said "All right."

PHIL
Well, that's that.

PEGGY
Oh, dear!

ROOSEVELT

(*A deep, deep sigh*)

I guess I'm not a very good President.

PEGGY

Oh, yes, you are, Mr. Roosevelt.

PHIL

Of course you are.

PEGGY

You mustn't be discouraged.

ROOSEVELT

(*Sadly*)

Well, it's my second term.

PHIL

But you've been a marvelous President. Everybody says so.

ROOSEVELT

No, they don't—they say terrible things. Ever read the *Herald Tribune*, or the *Baltimore Sun*, the *St. Louis Post-Dispatch*, the *Louisville Courier?* . . . Even the *New York Times*. . . .

PEGGY

Oh, what do you care what newspapers say?

ROOSEVELT

But they used to be so nice to me. I'll show you my scrapbook some time—you can see the difference.

PHIL

But the *people* like you. That's what counts. Look at those election returns the last time!

ROOSEVELT

(*Shaking his head*)

That was all Jim Farley. He could have elected Parkyakarkus.

PEGGY

Now, that's not true. I voted for you—for you, *yourself*.

ROOSEVELT

Thank you, Peggy.

PHIL

And so did I. And I know at least six other people who did, too.

ROOSEVELT

Thank you, Phil. Maybe I'll feel better after a while. . . . Haven't got a piece of chewing gum, have you?

PHIL

I could run and get you some.

ROOSEVELT

No, don't bother. I don't really want it, anyhow.

(There enters an elderly, distinguished-looking lady followed by a butler in full regalia, carrying a huge, elaborate cake)

THE LADY

Why, hello, Franklin! What are you doing here?

ROOSEVELT

Oh, hello, Mother.

MRS. ROOSEVELT

I thought you were making a Fourth of July speech.

ROOSEVELT

I'm going to later. Mother, I want you to meet two young friends of mine, Phil and Peggy. This is my mother.
(An exchange of courtesies)
Two of the nicest young people I ever met, Mother.

MRS. ROOSEVELT

Well, I'm sure I'm very glad to meet them. . . .
(Ever the mother)
What do you think of my son being President of the United States?

PEGGY

It's wonderful.

ROOSEVELT

Now, Mother.

66

MRS. ROOSEVELT

Twice, too.

ROOSEVELT

Mother—everybody knows I'm President of the United States.

MRS. ROOSEVELT

That's all right—doesn't do any harm to tell 'em. . . . I'm on the way to your Birthday Ball, Franklin.
(*Addressing* PEGGY)
You know, they give them all the time. Isn't that a beautiful cake?

PEGGY

It's lovely.

MRS. ROOSEVELT

Yes, I always bake them myself. . . . Well, we'll be late if we don't hurry.
(*She turns to the butler*)
Come on, Mr. Landon—hurry up!
(*And off they go*)

PEGGY

(*Stunned*)
Landon?

PHIL

Was that *the* Mr. Landon that ran for President?

ROOSEVELT

Yes, and he's the best butler we ever had.

67

PEGGY

Think of that!

ROOSEVELT

(*Thoughtfully*)

You know, I wonder if he'd have done any better if he'd got in.

THE CHIEF JUSTICE

(*Popping up behind a bush*)

Much better!

ROOSEVELT

(*Streaking it off after the justice*)

Why, you . . .

PEGGY

Mr. Roosevelt, don't go away. Mr. Roosevelt. . . .

(*A businesslike man strides in, carrying a bulging briefcase, into which he is dipping as he enters*)

THE MAN

(*Confronting* PHIL *and* PEGGY, *and pulling out a card*)

Peggy Jones?

PEGGY

Yes.

THE MAN

Philip Barker?

PHIL

Yes.

THE MAN

(*Handing each of them a card*)

Social Security cards.

PEGGY

Thank you.

THE MAN

Don't lose them—they'll be very valuable when you're sixty-five years old.

(*He is off again, consulting his list as he goes*)

Walter Bernstein, Harold Levinson, Sigrid Neilson. . . .

PHIL

(*Looking at the card*)

Well, this solves everything. Sixty-five! We only have forty years to wait and we won't have a thing to worry about.

> (*And into a song they go—a lyric celebrating the somewhat doubtful pleasures of being sixty-five years old. But, as they sing it, you are almost convinced that sixty-five is a highly desirable age. When it is over we see the* CHIEF JUSTICE *streaking it across the bridge, hotly pursued by* MR. ROOSEVELT. *The latter gives up the chase, but not completely—taking a bean shooter out of his pocket, he carefully lets go at the retreating Justice. And at this moment* MCINTYRE *comes on to announce that the* CABINET *is returning.* MR. ROOSEVELT *guiltily gets rid of the bean shooter and*

69

pulls himself together. And on stalks the CABINET, *all excitement*)

MORGENTHAU

Mr. President, we have found a way to balance the budget.

ROOSEVELT

No!

MORGENTHAU

Yes!

PEGGY

You see, l told you you mustn't be discouraged.

PHIL

There you are!

ROOSEVELT

Why, that's wonderful. Gentlemen, take your places— the Cabinet is in session. Come on, gentlemen—I can hardly wait. What is it?

MORGENTHAU

Mr. President, Phil and Peggy: When those women chased us out of here, we just went back and thought and thought. We were all pretty discouraged, so we went and saw the Marx Brothers picture. By the way, Frank, Harpo has got a scene in there . . .

(*He essays a Harpo Marx face*)

ROOSEVELT

Henry, for God's sake!

70

MORGENTHAU

All right—all right. Here it is.

FARLEY

Really, when you hear it, Frank—it's so simple. . . .

HULL

You'll die.

ROOSEVELT

(*Impatient*)

All right! What *is* it?

MORGENTHAU

(*Lowering his voice*)

Gold.

ROOSEVELT

Gold?

THE ENTIRE CABINET

Gold.

ROOSEVELT

What do you mean, gold?

MORGENTHAU

We mean all that gold that we've been buying from South Africa, and Russia, and God knows where!

ROOSEVELT

Well?

MORGENTHAU

Well, for years and years we've been buying all this gold. Remember—we built a place for it, down in Kentucky?

ROOSEVELT

Oh, yes—I saw a picture of it in the "March of Time."

MORGENTHAU

That's it. In Fort Knox. We built a great big place for it.

ROOSEVELT

Is it still there?

MORGENTHAU

Sure it is—the Army's watching it.

ROOSEVELT

That's good. . . . Go ahead, Henry—I'm all excited.

MORGENTHAU

Well, there must be billions down there by this time. *So* . . .

FARLEY

All we've got to do is to take it *out* of there . . .

MORGENTHAU

Bring it to Washington . . .

FARLEY

Balance the budget with it . . .

MORGENTHAU

And Phil and Peggy get married!

FARLEY

See?

MORGENTHAU

(*Climaxing the whole thing*)

Just as simple as that. What do you say?

ROOSEVELT

(*Quieting the excited* CABINET)

Now, wait a minute, wait a minute. I won't say this doesn't sound good, but let me get hold of the idea for a minute.

FARLEY

It's so easy, Frank. There it is, down there in a hole in the ground, not doing anybody any good.

ROOSEVELT

Well, just let me get it straight.

MORGENTHAU

Let me explain it, Mr. President. In South Africa, for instance, they dig the gold out of the ground, and sell it. Twenty-one dollars an ounce. But we said "No—we won't pay you twenty-one dollars an ounce; we'll pay you thirty-five dollars an ounce."

ROOSEVELT

We said that?

MORGENTHAU

Sure.

ROOSEVELT

We must have been crazy. Who did that?

MORGENTHAU

(*Embarrassed*)
Well—ah—you did.

ROOSEVELT

Me?

MORGENTHAU

Yes, Mr. President.

ROOSEVELT

Well, for goodness' sake! Why didn't somebody stop me?

FARLEY

Well, we didn't want to say anything at the time.

HULL

I believe you had a slight cold.

MISS PERKINS

And, besides, you had Congress back of you then.

ROOSEVELT

Look, Frances—why don't you toddle off to bed? . . . Go on, Henry.

MORGENTHAU

Well, that's really all there is to it, Mr. President. They take it out of a hole in the ground over there, and we buy it and put it in another hole in the ground here.

ROOSEVELT

That's all we do with it?

MORGENTHAU

That's all.

ROOSEVELT

It doesn't make much sense, does it? There must be some reason why we do that, isn't there?

MORGENTHAU

No. No reason at all. In fact, I once asked about it.

ROOSEVELT

You're sure it's not a sinking fund or something—for the American Legion?

MORGENTHAU

Positive.

FARLEY

Come on, Frank—what's there to think about?

ROOSEVELT

Now, don't rush me, Jim. . . .
(*Thinking aloud, pacing*)

75

Nothing to do with the American Legion—just lying
there in a hole in the ground . . .

(*Suddenly he comes to a decision*)

. . . Gentlemen, I'll do it!

(*A roar of approval from the* CABINET. *"Bully
for you, Mr. President!" . . . "That's great!" . . .
"Wonderful!" . . . "That's the old Franklin!"*)

PEGGY

At last, Phil!

PHIL

Peggy!

ROOSEVELT

McIntyre, listen to this. You know all that gold we've
got buried down in Fort Knox, Kentucky?

McINTYRE

Yes, sir.

ROOSEVELT

Well, I want you to get on the phone and tell them
to bring it to Washington immediately. Got that?

McINTYRE

(*Flying off*)

Yes, sir.

ROOSEVELT

(*His voice rising above the hubbub of excitement*)

Phil, Peggy—it gives me great pleasure to tell you that
your troubles are over. We are going to balance the
budget.

76

I'D RATHER BE RIGHT

(A cheer from the CABINET—*and that seems to be all the President needs. Unable to contain himself, he bursts into song—a song called, appropriately enough, "We're Going to Balance the Budget")*

Shoot your cameras,
Fly your flags,
Loosen up your money bags,
Spread the good news throughout the land,
Open that mike up
And strike up the band.

Tune up, bluebird, you're going to sing!
Swing out, church-bells, you're going to ring!
Take aim, Cupid, you're gonna go "Bing!"
We're going to balance the budget!
Cheer up, farmer, you'll buy a new car!
Wake up, landlord, and open the bar.
Come out, rainbow, wherever you are!
We're going to balance the budget!
Ta—Ta—Ra!
Hear the horn of plenty blow!
Ta—Ta—Ra!
The dollar bills will flow!
Yankee-Doodle, we're letting you know
We're going to balance the budget!

(And on comes the whole park crowd, singing and dancing. Victory at last!)

(Just at its height the celebration is brought to a sudden halt by the entrance of a gang of newsboys. "Extra! Extra! Stock market crash! Wall Street panic!")

ROOSEVELT

Wait a minute, everybody!
(The crowd is silent as newspapers are passed around)
"Panic in Wall Street. Stocks Crash Fifty Points as Government Moves Gold."

PHIL

"Pandemonium Reigns as Stock Market Collapses."

PEGGY

"Wall Street Paralyzed as Government Moves Gold."

ROOSEVELT

Oh, my goodness!

McINTYRE

They hadn't even moved it, Mr. President. They'd just opened the door.

ROOSEVELT

Oh, dear!

MORGENTHAU

I can't understand it.

ROOSEVELT

Me neither. You open a door in Kentucky and stocks drop fifty points in New York.

FARLEY

(*Thoroughly scared*)

Frank, we can't fool around with Wall Street. To hell with the country!

ROOSEVELT

(*Stunned*)

But what has that gold in a hole in the ground in Kentucky got to do with the stock market in New York?

MORGENTHAU

I don't know, but we'd better put it back, Mr. President. We'd better put it right back.

ROOSEVELT

(*Sadly*)

Yes, I suppose so. . . . Tell them to close the door, McIntyre.

MCINTYRE

(*Crushed*)

Yes, sir.

(MCINTYRE *goes. The music picks up again, but in funereal tempo*)

ROOSEVELT

(*Finally breaking the silence*)

Gee, and I had the wedding all planned. I was going

79

to give you your honeymoon on Vincent Astor's yacht, and I was going along for the fishing.

(PEGGY *begins to cry, softly*)

Don't cry, Peggy—don't cry. Everything will come out all right. I'm not unhappy. I'm not sad. Look.

(*And into a dance he goes—and what a dance! The crowd catches the contagion—the song picks up again. They sing as though their very hearts would burst—"We're Going to Balance the Budget!" It may not be true, but at the moment they believe it. The dancing and the singing reach a frenzied climax, flags are waving and horns are blowing, as*

THE CURTAIN DESCENDS

ACT TWO

ACT TWO

The scene is still Central Park, and apparently the problem is still unsolved. Anyhow, there sit MR. ROOSEVELT, PHIL *and* PEGGY, *still on that rock. There is only one small point of difference.* PEGGY *is asleep, her head resting on* MR. ROOSEVELT's *shoulder.*

PHIL

Mr. Roosevelt!

ROOSEVELT

Ssh! She's asleep.

PHIL

Oh!

ROOSEVELT

And she's having a nice dream, too. Look at that smile. I wonder what she's dreaming about.

PHIL

I'll bet I know what she's dreaming about. What we *both* dream about—a good deal. Our wedding, and the house we'd like to build, and the kids we'll have, and our whole life together. I dream about it myself—a lot.

(Whereupon, this being a musical show, the entire dream unfolds. It turns out to be quite an elaborate

83

ballet, depicting, as PHIL *had predicted, the marriage, homecoming, and general progress through life of a young American couple. Their children are born and grow to maturity; finally the* PHIL *and* PEGGY *of the ballet are old and sere—but still dancing, you may be sure of that.* PEGGY, *of course, sleeps blissfully through it all, for it is* her *dream. When it is all over she opens her eyes and stretches)*

PEGGY

Have—have I been asleep?

PHIL

You certainly have.

ROOSEVELT

I should say so. You got married, and had children, and everything.

PEGGY

Oh, Mr. Roosevelt! . . . Didn't anything happen? Is the budget balanced? I dreamed the budget was balanced.

ROOSEVELT

You dreamed the budget was balanced? Right on the rock?

PEGGY

Yes, I did.

ROOSEVELT

Get out of the way, Phil.

(And he lies down on the rock, hopefully)

84

(Before anything can happen, however, a P.W.A. group enters the scene—but a P.W.A. group expensively tricked out in broadcloth shirts, silk overalls. And who is at the head of it but our old friend, MR. MAXWELL)

PHIL

(Considerably surprised)

Mr. Maxwell, are you working for the P.W.A.?

(To ROOSEVELT)

You remember Mr. Maxwell, my boss?

ROOSEVELT

Oh, yes. You're not in the balloon business any more, huh?

MAXWELL

No, indeed. I'm in a wonderful business now. Government employee! And for the first time, Mr. Roosevelt, I am keeping what I make. Only twenty-three dollars and eighty-six cents a week, Mr. Roosevelt, but it's *all mine.* You don't get any of it, not even the eighty-six cents. And permit me to introduce a little group of happy Government employees—J. W. Bragdon, President of the American Steel Corporation; H. L. Dennison, United Woolen Mills; Courtney Leland, American Railroads; D. A. Sampson, International Copper Company, and Matthew W. Patterson, United Light and Power. Mr. Roosevelt.

I'D RATHER BE RIGHT

(*An exchange of greetings*)
All right, gentlemen—let's go to work.

(*With an elaborate cluttering of picks and shovels,
a very small twig is picked up, transferred from
one man to another, and finally deposited about
ten feet from where it started. And at the same
time, to ease the burden of their labor, they sing*)

We work all day
For the P.W.A.
Let the market crash,
We collect our cash;
We sing as we work,
And we work as we sing:

"Skit-skat Beety-o!
Skit-skat Beety-o!"
Labor is the thing, my lads—
Labor is the thing.

At twelve o'clock, when the whistle blows "lunch,"
We scram to the Colony with the bunch.
At three o'clock we always arrange
To get our reports from the Exchange.
At six o'clock we go to the club—
A guy who works needs a steam and a rub.
While drying off, we sing:

86

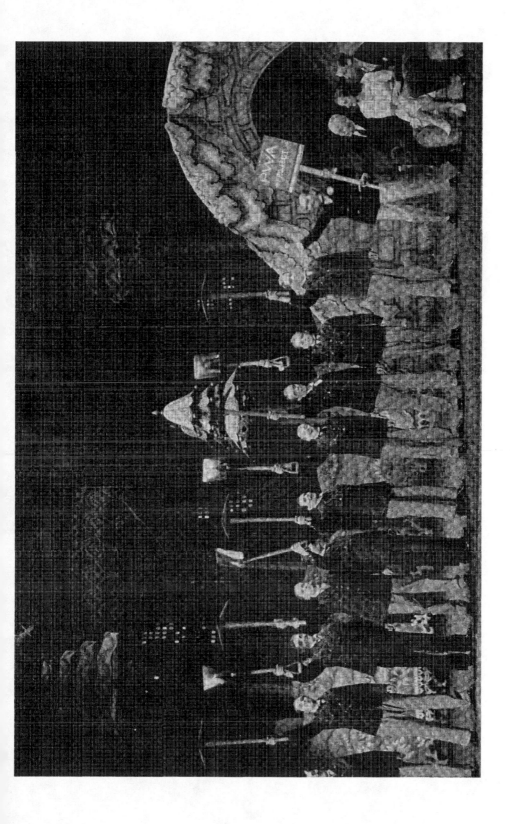

MR. ROOSEVELT MEETS A LITTLE GROUP OF HAPPY GOVERNMENT EM-
PLOYEES—J. W. BRAGDON, PRESIDENT OF THE AMERICAN STEEL
CORPORATION; H. L. DENNISON, UNITED WOOLEN MILLS; COURTNEY
LELAND, AMERICAN RAILROADS; D. A. SAMPSON, INTERNATIONAL
COPPER COMPANY, AND MATTHEW W. PATTERSON, UNITED LIGHT
AND POWER

I'D RATHER BE RIGHT

"Skit-skat Beety-o!
Skit-skat Beety-o!"
Labor is the thing, my lads—
Labor is the thing!

The Union workingman's homeward trend
Is toward Fifth Avenue or East End.
A union man must leave home to vote—
A meeting's been called on Vanderbilt's boat.
At last the nervous breakdown comes—
We go to Federal sanitariums,
To cut out dolls and sing.

(*And once more the chorus. That over, they are a
pretty tired bunch of men. But they summon up
enough energy to take themselves on to the next
job, where, probably, they will dig up a dandelion.
For it must be remembered that this is not an
ordinary group of P.W.A. workers, but the very
rich, soldiering on the job, as usual. At all events,
they go.* MR. ROOSEVELT *barely has time to look
reproachfully after them when there is a new in-
terruption. A little boy and girl of eight or ten,
this time, running excitedly in with cries of
"Grandpa!"*)

ROOSEVELT
Why, it's Sistie and Buzzie. What are you doing here?
. . . These are my grandchildren, Sistie and Buzzie.

87

SISTIE

Grandpa—the man won't let us go on the merry-go-round.

ROOSEVELT

Of course he will. What are you talking about?

BUZZIE

It isn't going.

SISTIE

There's a strike or something.

ROOSEVELT

A strike on the merry-go-round?

(*And there enter two Italians, of the traditional big-mustached sort. The first of them,* TONY *by name, is struggling into his coat. He is quickly followed by* JOE, *arguing as he comes*)

TONY

No, no. I quitta the job. You no pay me more money, I quitta the job. That's all—you getta somebody else.

BUZZIE

Grandpa, make 'em turn the merry-go-round. We want to ride.

ROOSEVELT

Just a minute. What seems to be the trouble?

(JOE *and* TONY *both start to explain at once—a flood of broken English*)

Now, wait a minute. One at a time. What's *your* name?

TONY

Tony.

ROOSEVELT

All right, Tony. You speak first.

TONY

He's-a my boss. He owna the merry-go-round. Las' week he say, "Turn 'em more fast. Speed 'em up, Tony. Speed 'em up." All right, I speed 'em up. So I say— "Boss, if I speed 'em up, I wanta more money." He say no—so I quit.

JOE

Tony, I cannota pay you more money.

(*He turns to* ROOSEVELT)

Sure I say, "Speed 'em up, Tony." If he no speed 'em up, I no maka money.

ROOSEVELT

(*Blandly*)

Well, now—this is very simple. It so happens we've just passed a law in this country to cover exactly this kind of thing. It's called the Wagner Act. And we'll have your merry-go-round going in two minutes, with both of you very happy and satisfied.

JOE

Ah! You gonna fix, huh?

TONY

That's-a good.

JOE

(*To the children*)
He fixa—we giva you beeg free ride.
(*The children jump up and down with delight*)

TONY

Si, si—beeg free ride!

ROOSEVELT

That's the true American spirit. We'll have this fixed
in no time.
(*He calls*)
McIntyre! Oh, McIntyre!
(MCINTYRE *appears*)

MCINTYRE

Yes, Mr. President?

ROOSEVELT

I want to see the Wagner Act.

MCINTYRE

(*Calling off*)
The Wagner Act!

(There is a voice in the far distance: "The Wagner Act!")

(A blast of music, and on come two large German acrobats, fully tricked out with dumbbells, weights, etc. Oblivious to everything, they at once start to go into their act—lifting, grunting, calling to one another in the manner of acrobats. Roosevelt watches this for one puzzled second, then realizes that something is wrong. He tries to make himself heard above the din)

ROOSEVELT

Hold on there a second, please! Just a minute, if you please! Please! Please! McIntyre! McIntyre! Stop just a second, please!

(Finally gaining a little quiet)

McIntyre, have you gone crazy? I asked to see the Wagner Act.

McIntyre

This is the Wagner Act, sir. Hans and Fritz Wagner— Federal Theatre Project No. 34268.

ROOSEVELT

No, no—McIntyre! Listen . . . The Wagner Labor Relations Act. It's a law, McIntyre—a law. And I want to see a copy of it.

McIntyre

(Disappearing)

O-o-o-o-h!

ROOSEVELT
(*To the* ACROBATS)
I'm very sorry—there's been a little mistake.

THE ACROBATS
Wass iss?

ROOSEVELT
There's been a *mistake*. We didn't want to see *you*. It's something else.

BUZZIE
But, Grandpa—*we* want to see them.

SISTIE
We like them.

ROOSEVELT
Well, maybe they'll do it somewhere else for you.
    (*To the Germans*)
You don't mind, do you?

THE ACROBATS
Sure, sure. We do it any place. Government pay us!
    (*And off they go, followed by the happy* SISTIE *and* BUZZIE)

McINTYRE
(*Re-entering with a huge legal manuscript*)
Here you are, sir. Here it is.

ROOSEVELT

Ah, that's better. Here we are. The Wagner Act.

JOE

Ah, now he's-a goin' to fix. You listen, Tony.

TONY

Okay.

ROOSEVELT

Just give me a chance to glance at this—I've never seen it before.

(*Skimming through the papers*)

Ah—just a minute. "Congress of the United States." . . . Ah, here we are. Now, then. . . . You are the employer and you are the employee!

JOE

What's-a that?

ROOSEVELT

Well, you're the boss, and he works for you.

TONY

That's-a right.

ROOSEVELT

All right. Now, under the Wagner Act, you have got to recognize each other.

(*To* JOE)

Do you recognize Tony?

JOE

Sure I recognize him. He worka for me eleven years.
Hello, Tony.

TONY

Hello, Boss.
(*They shake hands*)

JOE

(*To* ROOSEVELT)
Okay?

ROOSEVELT

(*Uncertainly*)
I suppose so. That's what it says here.
(*To* PHIL)
Seems kind of funny, doesn't it?

PHIL

(*Politely*)
Yes, it does.

ROOSEVELT

Well! Let's see what else it says. I know it's supposed
to fix everything. The Supreme Court almost didn't pass
it, just on that account. Ah—here we are. "Pursuant to
recognition, the employer and employee then bargain
collectively." Oh, yes—collective bargaining. You two
have got to bargain collectively.

JOE

How we do that?

94

ROOSEVELT

I'll show you. . . . Tony, do you represent a majority of his employees?

TONY

(*After thinking this over*)

No. Just me.

ROOSEVELT

No, no. Listen. You are *most* of the people who work for him, aren't you?

TONY

(*It's entirely too much for him*)

All I wanta is more money.

ROOSEVELT

All right, all right. But the point is, you are going to speak *for* yourself, aren't you?

TONY

Sure I speaka for myself. Who you think I am, Charlie McCarthy?

ROOSEVELT

Well, I wouldn't be surprised! Anyhow, this is where you bargain collectively. You tell him what you want, and you tell him what you'll give.

TONY

That's-a easy. I wanta more money.

I'D RATHER BE RIGHT

JOE
(*With great definiteness*)
I no give it to you.

TONY
Okay.

JOE
(*Putting it right up to* ROOSEVELT)
Whata we do now?

ROOSEVELT
(*Thinking it over*)
Say, maybe the Supreme Court passed this just for spite.

JOE
Hey, Boss, I thoughta you fix.

ROOSEVELT
Well, this is a new law, you know. It takes a little time
for it to work.

TONY
He's-a no fix, he's-a no fix.

ROOSEVELT
Now, wait a minute, Tony. Let me put it this way.
Suppose *you* owned the merry-go-round, and *he* was
working for *you*. You'd feel different, wouldn't you?

TONY
If I owna merry-go-round, I give him everything he
ask for.

96

ROOSEVELT
(*To* PHIL *and* PEGGY, *triumphantly*)
You see—that's the Wagner Act.

JOE
All right—you so smart, Tony. I *giva* you the merry-go-round. I worka for you.

TONY
You meana that, Boss?

JOE
That's-a right. You be the boss; you paya me!

TONY
Okay.

JOE
All right. How mucha you pay me?

TONY
Just whata you pay me!

JOE
Oh, no. I wanta more money.

TONY
I cannota *pay* you more money.

JOE
You no pay me more money, I quit.

97

I'D RATHER BE RIGHT

TONY

I quit, too.

JOE

All right, we both quit.

ROOSEVELT

You both quit?

TONY

We both quit.

JOE

What we do now? What we do with the merry-go-round?

ROOSEVELT

You both quit.

JOE

What's-a matter? You no understand English?

ROOSEVELT

I understand English all right, but maybe the Wagner Act should have been written in Italian. . . . Now, wait a minute.

(*He pages through*)

Oh, dear. The Government takes it over!

JOE

(*Delighted*)

We worka for the Government now?

ROOSEVELT

I'm afraid so.

98

JOE

Tony! We worka for the Government! That meansa we're rich!

(*And away they go, chattering happily in Italian*)

ROOSEVELT

(*The Wagner Act still in his hand, he considers for a moment what to do with it—then gets an idea*)

Well, we'll put it with Mr. Lippmann.

(*And he does*)

PHIL

Look, Mr. Roosevelt—we're taking up a lot of your time. You've got to write that speech and everything. Perhaps Peggy and I had better go.

ROOSEVELT

Now, you'll do no such thing. Why, if you went away now, I'd feel terrible. I'd feel just awful.

PEGGY

Well, if you feel that way, Mr. Roosevelt, we won't go.

ROOSEVELT

Because what I'm trying to do for you two is right. *Dead* right. And I'll tell you something. I'd rather be right than President.

(*He thinks it over*)

No, I wouldn't. I'd rather be both.

(*And at this point* Mrs. Roosevelt *comes bustling through again, still accompanied by* Mr. Landon. *He is again carrying a birthday cake*)

Mrs. Roosevelt

Hello, Franklin.

Roosevelt

Hello, Mother. . . . You remember my little friends, Phil and Peggy.

Mrs. Roosevelt

Oh, yes—how do you do, my dear?

Roosevelt

How are you, Landon?

Landon

(*Heartily*)

I'm fine!

Mrs. Roosevelt

I'm on the way to your Birthday Ball, Franklin—I baked a cake again.

Roosevelt

That's splendid.

Mrs. Roosevelt

Oh, listen, Franklin—I had a letter from Mrs. Baxter . . .

(*She is pulling it out of her bag*)

. . . you know, the woman I met on that West Indies cruise. She lives in Buffalo. Listen:

"DEAR MRS. ROOSEVELT:—I do hate to bother you again, but Ruthie"—(that's Mrs. Baxter's daughter, Ruth Baxter—she goes to art school)—"Ruthie got another ticket yesterday for going past a red light. It really was not her fault, so I thought you would not mind asking your son to fix it for her. I know he's a pretty busy man these days, so please tell him it is not the two dollars, but if Ruthie has to go to Traffic Court she will be late for her art class, and they are very strict."

Here, Franklin.
(*She hands him the ticket*)

ROOSEVELT
(*Knowing that it is useless to argue*)
All right, Mother.

MRS. ROOSEVELT
Now, you'll do it right away, won't you? You won't forget?

ROOSEVELT
No, Mother. I won't forget.

MRS. ROOSEVELT

Because she was very nice—Mrs. Baxter. She voted for you. And she made her husband do it, too, even though he didn't want to.

ROOSEVELT

All right, Mother. I'll attend to it.

MRS. ROOSEVELT

What's the matter, Franklin? You're not yourself at all.

ROOSEVELT

I'm all right, Mother. Nothing's the matter.

MRS. ROOSEVELT

Now, Franklin—I can tell just by looking at you. What's the matter?

ROOSEVELT

Mother, it's nothing you could do anything about. It's —it's the budget.

MRS. ROOSEVELT

What about it?

ROOSEVELT
(*Wearily giving in*)
I can't balance it, Mother. I can't balance it. So there!

MRS. ROOSEVELT

Well, Franklin, you've *got* to balance it. You promised, didn't you?

ROOSEVELT

(*Evasively*)
Well—in a way . . .

MRS. ROOSEVELT

Franklin, a promise is a promise.

ROOSEVELT

(*Bursting out*)
But it isn't so easy, Mother, when you're President of the United States.

MRS. ROOSEVELT

There must be *some* way. Mr. Landon did it when he was Governor of Kansas—didn't you, Mr. Landon?
(*A slow smile comes over* MR. LANDON's *face*)
You balanced the budget in Kansas?

LANDON

(*Complacently*)
I did, Mrs. Roosevelt—I most certainly did.

MRS. ROOSEVELT

Look! Why can't Mr. Landon tell you how he balanced the budget in Kansas? Then you could do that with *your* budget.

ROOSEVELT

(*Only half catching this*)

Huh?

MRS. ROOSEVELT

Let Mr. Landon tell you how he balanced *his* budget
—then *you* do the same thing.

ROOSEVELT

Say, that's an idea. . . . How did you do it, Mr.
Landon?

LANDON

(*His moment of triumph at hand*)

Not a chance, Mr. Roosevelt! Not a chance!

ROOSEVELT

Oh, come now, Mr. Landon. I didn't mean those things
I said about you.

LANDON

Perhaps not, Mr. Roosevelt—but this makes up for a
good deal. It's true I didn't photograph well, nor did I
have that smile. And I will frankly admit that I was
lousy on the radio. But, Mr. Roosevelt, I balanced my
budget! So, as we say in Kansas, Mr. Roosevelt—try that
on your ukulele!

(*And he goes*)

MRS. ROOSEVELT

(*Running after him*)

Mr. Landon, you come right back! Aren't servants
terrible these days?

LANDON: "I WILL FRANKLY ADMIT THAT I WAS LOUSY ON THE RADIO, BUT, MR. ROOSEVELT, I BALANCED MY BUDGET"

I'D RATHER BE RIGHT

Roosevelt

(*A deep sigh*)

I wonder whose butler I'll be in a couple of years. . . .

Peggy

Oh, Mr. Roosevelt!

Roosevelt

You know, I like this job, being President. Confidentially, I'll tell you something.

(*And he does—in a song entitled "Off the Record"*)

It's really a wonderful job
For fellows like George, Abe, and me too.
It's great to shake hands with the mob,
And to hold every kid on your knee, too.
Every word that I speak goes into headlines;
When I speak, all the papers hold their deadlines
But I've found a way of dropping a hint,
Or a glint of the truth
That the boys cannot print.
For instance—
For instance—

When I was only Governor, and just a good-time-
    Charlie,
A certain party came to me—he said his name was
    Farley.
  Don't print this—it's strictly off the record.

105

He sat right down and talked to me till I was in a
    stupor,
And ended up by selling me the works of Fenimore
    Cooper—
    Don't print it; it's strictly off the record.
I said: "You're quite a salesman; you've been sent
    here by the fates;
If you can sell these dreary books, which everybody
    hates,
Then maybe you can sell *me* to the whole United
    States!"
    But that's off the record.

My messages to Congress are a lot of boola-boola;
I'm not so fond of Bankhead, but I'd love to meet
    Tallulah.
    Don't print it; it's strictly off the record.
I sit up in my bedroom reading books like Silas
    Marner,
And Sears and Roebuck catalogues to get away from
    Garner.
    Don't print it; it's strictly off the record.
If I'm not re-elected and the worst comes to the worst,
I'll never die of hunger and I'll never die of thirst.
I've got one boy with Dupont and another one with
    Hearst—
    But that's off the record.

When I go up to Hyde Park, it is not just for the ride
    there; *106*

It's not that I love Hyde Park, but I love to park
    and hide there.
    Don't print that; it's strictly off the record.
Oh, sing a song of Boulder Dam, but what's a little
    song worth?
We'll use it to throw razor blades, and maybe Alice
    Longworth.
    Don't print it; it's strictly off the record.
And now I'd like to talk about some folks I used
    to know—
Mr. John L. Lewis and his famous C.I.O.
"Frankie and Johnnie were sweethearts"—
    But that's off the record.

My speeches on the radio have made me quite a hero,
I only have to say "My Friends" and stocks go down
    to zero.
    Don't print it; it's strictly off the record.
The radio officials say that I'm the leading fellow—
Jack Benny can be President and I'll go on for Jello.
    Don't print it; it's strictly off the record.
It's pleasant at the White House, but I'll tell you how
    I feel:
The food is something terrible—just sauerkraut and
    veal;
If Eleanor would stay at home, I'd get a decent
    meal—
    But that's off the record.

(*After which the* CABINET *re-enters. They are not very happy*)

Ah, here we are! Gentlemen, the Cabinet is in session. Now, what about balancing the budget? Have you thought of anything?

FARLEY
What's the use of kidding ourselves, Frank? We could sit here till next week and not get anywhere.

ROOSEVELT
We've *got* to get somewhere. I told Phil and Peggy I was going to get them married if it was the last thing I did as President. And I'm going to do it if it takes me ten years.

FARLEY
Yes, but you haven't got ten years, Frank. The time is getting kind of short.

ROOSEVELT
Well, we've got to do something for Phil and Peggy, and all the rest like them.

FARLEY
But there you are, Frank—we've just got so much time.

ROOSEVELT
Boys, we need *more* time. You know what it looks

like to me, to give us a real chance? Hang on to your hats now. A *third term!*

(*A long, low whistle from the* CABINET. *They look at one another, each afraid to trust his own thoughts*)

Yes, sir, a third . . .

(ROOSEVELT *suddenly remembers those boys behind the rocks and bushes. He looks around apprehensively, but they aren't there. He finishes his sentence with some relief*)

A third term . . . It's the only way out, boys. What do you say?

HULL

A third term!

MORGENTHAU

But do you think it can be done? It never has, you know.

HULL

Nobody's *ever* had a third term, not since George Washington said no.

ROOSEVELT

All right—Washington said no, but has that got to stand forever? Besides, how do you know *why* he said no? He was probably having trouble with his teeth— it may have been just as simple as that. Anyway, I'm sure that if George Washington had known Phil and Peggy, he'd have said yes.

MORGENTHAU

Well, we'd *all* like to help Phil and Peggy.

HULL

Of course we would!

MORGENTHAU

But a third term . . . Can it be done?

ROOSEVELT

It can, and I'll tell you how. . . . McIntyre! Bring me
another fireside!

FARLEY

No, no, Frank. You'll never swing this with a fireside
talk. . . . This is too big.

ROOSEVELT

Boys, I don't like to override you, but this time I must.
I'm going on the air.

(*There is a pause*)

FARLEY

Your mind's made up, Frank?

ROOSEVELT

Absolutely.

FARLEY

Then you've got to do it right. Believe me, Frank—
just a fireside talk isn't enough. When Lucky Strikes go

on the air, they don't just talk about the cigarette. They give 'em entertainment first—a good band, comedy. And that's what *we've* got to do. Music, jokes. *Then* you go on with the commercial.

HULL

He's right, Frank.

MISS PERKINS

That's so.

MORGENTHAU

It's the only way you'll do it.

ROOSEVELT

All right—if that's the only way. Let's get the greatest array of talent that's ever been heard on the air.

FARLEY

There *isn't* anybody. Between movies and the radio, there isn't anybody left. We've got to do it ourselves, Frank.

MORGENTHAU

That's a good idea—let's do it ourselves.

HULL

All right.

FARLEY

Henry, you've got a voice. I hear you crooning every day, all over the Treasury Department.

MORGENTHAU

Oh, I just croon a little for my secretary.

FARLEY

That's all right—you'll go on. . . . Cordell, you can tell jokes. . . . Frances, Washington gossip. . . . Now, the big thing is the band—we need a band.

SWANSON

What about us? We can play.

FARLEY

Marvelous! Do you do swing? Can you carve it out?

ROPER

Nothing else but!

FARLEY

All right, boys! Get your instruments!

(*And they do. Drums, piano, trombone, everything. And immediately a radio announcer comes along with a microphone*)

ANNOUNCER

Through the courtesy of Kirkman's Laundry Soap, which has generously relinquished its time, you will now hear a new program. Allow me to introduce Postmaster-General James A. Farley. All right, Mr. Farley, you're on.

(FARLEY *at once steps to the microphone*)

112

FARLEY

Good evening, everybody! This is your Master of Ceremonies, Postmaster-General Farley, on the air with our new program—WHITE HOUSE HOTEL, featuring FRANKLIN D. ROOSEVELT and all the lads. Every week at this time, we invite you to gather round the White House fireside, and join us in our White House Jamboree. We open tonight's program with Franklin D. Roosevelt's Hillbilly Swing Orchestra. Let 'er go, boys!

> (*And they do. A medley of American airs done to swing.* FARLEY *rushes to the microphone when it is over*)

Yowsah, yowsah! Those boys can certainly carve it out, can't they, folks? And remember, they are just as hot *in* the Cabinet. . . . And now, folks, your Master of Ceremonies will endeavor to amuse you with a few jokes right out of the Dead Letter Office—ha, ha! Assisted by that delightful, delirious diplomat, the Secretary of State.

> (MR. HULL *walks to the microphone*)

Well, Mr. Secretary, and how is everything over at the State Department?

HULL

Fine, Jim—just fine! Funny thing happened, though. I was sitting in my office the other day when a couple of Irishmen came in—Pat and Mike.

FARLEY

Boy, you kill me—Pat and Mike.

113

(*He indicates that the others should laugh with him—which they do, uproariously*)
Go on, Mr. Secretary—Pat and Mike came into the State Department. What happened?

HULL

Well, Mike comes over to me and says: "For the love of God, man, can you give me a new passport?" And I says, "What became of your old passport, Mike?" "Well," says Mike, "I had it in the kitchen and my wife Bridget fed it to the pig."

FARLEY

And what happened to the pig?

HULL

"Well," says Mike, "the pig took the next boat to Ireland!"
(*Hilarious laughter.* MR. FARLEY *cuts it off—the studio trick*)

FARLEY

Thank you, folks. . . . And now some spicy bits of Washington gossip, dished out by that dimpled darling of the Cabinet, the Secretary of Labor.

MISS PERKINS
(*As the man at the drums works the telegrapher's key, à la Winchell*)
Washington, D. C.—FLASH: What Congresswoman is expecting a bundle from Heaven, but is meanwhile keep-

114

ing her seat in Congress? . . . Fashion note: Senator William E. Borah, the stormy petrel of the U. S. Senate, sleeps in just his pajama tops. . . . Orchids to Congressman Sol Bloom, who sent out enough seeds last year to be elected till 1960. . . . One of the beds that George Washington once slept in was occupied by a couple of other people a few nights ago. Guess who! . . . What former President of the United States, now living in Southern California, still owes the Washington Hand Laundry a dollar and sixty-five cents?

FARLEY
Thank you, Frances, thank you. And now it is my pleasure to introduce to you that merry mathematical fool, the Secretary of the Treasury.
(MR. MORGENTHAU *comes to the microphone*)

FARLEY
What are you going to sing for us tonight, Henry?

MORGENTHAU
Jim, I want to sing a brand new number for the folks listening in tonight. A little song entitled, "A Baby Bond for Baby."
(*À la Crosby, he croons into the mike*)
This is Secretary Morgenthau, folks—singing to you on the White House Jamboree.

I'll tell the microphone I love you,
That's worse than writing, "I love you, dear,"

And by the stratosphere above you,
I'll swear forever to be true, dear.
I won't buy you perfume, I won't buy a ring;
I've a token of affection that means more than
    anything.

It's just
A baby bond for baby—
Take it, tootsie, with my love;
Papa's glad to dig down deep for baby.
A bunch of roses may be
Old and faded in a day,
But a baby bond will keep for baby.

Please remember,
In December,
There may be a storm;
Bonds are only scraps of paper,
But, by gosh, they'll keep you warm.
Baby love your baby, and I'll promise that I'll
    buy
Another baby bond for baby
Bye and bye!

FARLEY
(*Cutting off applause after song*)
    Now, if you want to hear Henry sing your favorite song next week, just send in the name of it along with definite proof that you are a registered Democrat.

(*His tone changes completely*)
And now, ladies and gentlemen of the radio audience
—we bring to you the star of tonight's program—the
greatest personality on the air today—that grand old pal
of the air-waves—FRANKLIN D. ROOSEVELT!

(*Wild applause. The band goes into a swing ver-
sion of "Happy Days Are Here Again." Mr.
ROOSEVELT steps to the microphone; stands there
smiling until the music and the applause die down*)

ROOSEVELT

My friends! I am not going to try to be funny tonight,
because what I am going to ask you to do is not very
funny. But first, I want to introduce to you two young
friends of mine, who can perhaps explain, better than I
can, the purpose of this White House Jamboree. Miss
Peggy Jones and Mr. Philip Barker.
(PHIL *and* PEGGY *appear a trifle surprised*)

(*Whispering to them*)
Sing your song. The way you did it for the Cabinet.

(*And they do so. A reprise of the "Have You Met
Miss Jones?" of all things*)

(MR. ROOSEVELT *returns to the microphone*)
My friends, the reason I asked you to listen to that
little love song is that those two young folks are in love.
And I've made them a promise that I will see them mar-

ried and happy . . . but alas! my friends, that takes time.
More time, I am afraid, than I shall have. And so I am
asking the American people, who have always believed
in love and marriage, to give me time to bring these two
young loving hearts together, to give me time to weld
as one these star-crossed lovers, to give me—a third term.
You've given me two terms—give me one more. Think
what you get, folks. A balanced budget, some great radio
programs, and anything I can think up during my third
term. So, be sure to listen in next week at this same hour,
to hear Jim and Cordell, Frances and Henry, the Hillbilly Swing Band, and the latest news of Phil and Peggy
and my third term.

> (*He is about to sign off when the* ANNOUNCER
> *presses a paper into his hand.* MR. ROOSEVELT *con-
> sults it; turns again to the microphone*)

I am asked to remind you that Lady Esther's Face
Powder is on sale at all neighborhood drug stores.

> (*And the program is ended. As was the case with
> the beauty appeal, the answer comes quickly. On
> walk the nine members of the Supreme Court.
> They are carrying radios, so be prepared for the
> worst*)

THE CHIEF JUSTICE

We heard that, Mr. President. And we are very sorry
to inform you that you cannot run for a third term. It is
unconstitutional.

ROOSEVELT

Don't give me that. The Constitution doesn't say a word about it. I know my Constitution.

THE CHIEF JUSTICE

Oh, you do, do you? Well, Mr. President, the Court has just been in session, and we have just declared the Constitution unconstitutional. . . . How do you like that?

ROOSEVELT

That's fine. That's all we needed. So now the Constitution is unconstitutional, huh? Tell me something—is there anything left in this country that still *is* constitutional?

THE CHIEF JUSTICE

Yes. The Supreme Court. . . . Come on, Justice Black. Don't forget you're explaining everything again at seven-thirty.

(*And they go*)

ROOSEVELT

(*To the* CABINET)

Boys, you look kind of tired—why don't you go home? See if your wives are still constitutional.

(*So they do.* ROOSEVELT *turns again to the youngsters*)

I don't need to tell you I'm sorry, kids. I did everything I could.

PEGGY

We know, Mr. Roosevelt.

PHIL

You know, it's funny, isn't it? All this business about the whole country, and balancing the budget. You wouldn't think it would touch Peggy and me, but I guess it does. And we want so little, Mr. Roosevelt. Just the right to work, and be married to each other—and—bring up our kids. We don't want much. If we could have just that. That isn't too much to ask, is it?

ROOSEVELT

No, Phil, it isn't. And in a great big country like this, you'd think you could have it. You've got a right to it. . . . Kids, you've given it to me—that's my Fourth of July speech . . . I'm ready, McIntyre!
(*The orchestra strikes up "Dixie" and a gay Fourth of July crowd comes promptly on. At the same time, a speaker's stand, with American flags draped around it, is brought on for* MR. ROOSEVELT)

ROOSEVELT

(*Mounting the platform*)
You know, a President has to make an awful lot of speeches. Some of them are fun, and some of them he just has to make because he's President. Now, you take the Fourth of July. A President always has to make a speech on the Fourth of July, and generally there's noth-

ing he can say, except that it's the Fourth of July, and hurray! But this time I've got something I want to say. You see, I know that people are kind of worried just now —they just don't know what's going to happen. I wish I could stand here today and tell you that there isn't any- thing to worry about. Well, that's not true. There *are* things to worry about, but I do know this: that this is too big and too fine a country to let anything lick it. We've come through a lot of troubles since that first Fourth of July. We fought for our freedom, we fought among ourselves, we've had bad Presidents and good Presidents; we've had panics and depressions and floods and strikes and wars. But it seems there's something in this country—a sort of spirit that holds us all together— that always sees us through. And we mustn't ever lose that. Just remember, folks, that even though things are a little wrong right now, we've got a chance to make 'em right, because at least this is a country where you can come out and *talk* about what's wrong. And there aren't many left like that nowadays. You know some- thing? It doesn't matter whether *I'm* President or any- body else is, and it never has mattered. That's not im- portant. There's only one thing that really matters in this country, or ever will.

(*With a wave of the hand, he indicates the multi- tude*)

You!

(*The crowd applauds, and the orchestra again plays "Dixie"*)

. (*He leans over and addresses* PHIL *and* PEGGY)

Phil, Peggy—you want my advice? Get married. Take your life and live it. You'll manage. People have done it before. You'll come through somehow. Listen—suppose I *don't* balance the budget? There'll be a baby born every minute, just the same. But I'll balance it! I'm not through trying—not by a darned sight!

(*And by way of proof he goes into the song again —"We're Going to Balance the Budget." Moreover, he seems to mean it. The crowd joins in.* ROOSEVELT *descends from the platform and marches, singing, up to the top of the bridge, the crowd cheering as he goes. Posed at the top point of the bridge, he turns to* PHIL *and* PEGGY)

ROOSEVELT

Good-bye, Phil! Good-bye, Peggy!

PHIL AND PEGGY

Good-bye, Mr. Roosevelt! Good-bye!

ROOSEVELT

Drop in and see me at the White House some time!

(*The crowd cheers again. With a jaunty farewell to the multitude, a final dance step—he goes. And suddenly the stage is black. Silent. Then slowly the lights come up again. The lighted windows of the buildings are shining in the background: in the distance the park concert is just coming to a finish. And there sit* PHIL *and* PEGGY, *just as we had left them. His head is in her lap, her arm around his shoulder. And then, with the stopping of the music, he suddenly wakes.* PEGGY *smiles at him*)

PEGGY

Have a nice nap, darling?

PHIL

I wasn't asleep.

PEGGY

Oh, yes, you were. I kissed you twice and you never moved.

PHIL

(*Abruptly*)

Peggy!

PEGGY

What?

PHIL

Let's get married—*tomorrow.*

PEGGY

Why, Phil! What's changed you?

PHIL

Never mind. Will you do it?

PEGGY

Sure I will, Phil. Darling!

(*They embrace. And that darned* POLICEMAN *comes back*)

123

I'D RATHER BE RIGHT

POLICEMAN

Hey! Where do you think you are? Russia?

PHIL

(*Light of heart*)

No, officer. We're in America, and doing very nicely, thank you!

CURTAIN

Printed in the United States
117998LV00006B/196-201/A

9 781417 992287